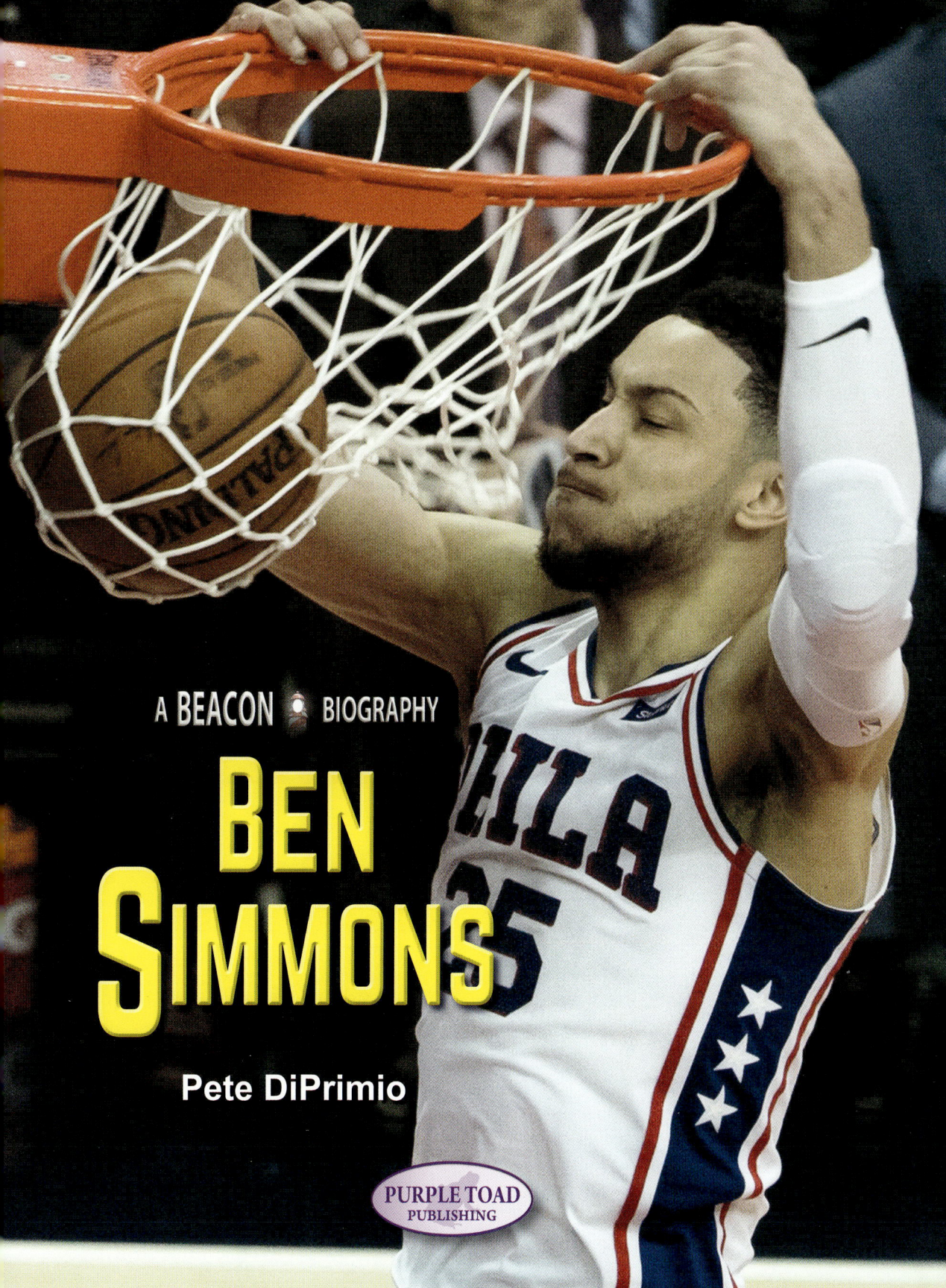

A BEACON BIOGRAPHY

Ben Simmons

Pete DiPrimio

PURPLE TOAD PUBLISHING

Copyright © 2019 by Purple Toad Publishing, Inc. All rights reserved. No part of this book may be reproduced without written permission from the publisher. Printed and bound in the United States of America.

Printing   1   2   3   4   5   6   7   8   9

A Beacon Biography

Angelina Jolie
Anthony Davis
Ben Simmons
Big Time Rush
Bill Nye
Cam Newton
Carly Rae Jepsen
Carson Wentz
Chadwick Boseman
Daisy Ridley
Drake
Ed Sheeran
Ellen DeGeneres
Elon Musk
Ezekiel Elliott
Gal Gadot
Harry Styles of One Direction
Jennifer Lawrence
Joel Embiid
John Boyega

Kevin Durant
Lorde
Malala
Maria von Trapp
Markus "Notch" Persson
Meghan Markle
Michelle Obama
Millie Bobby Brown
Misty Copeland
Mo'ne Davis
Muhammad Ali
Neil deGrasse Tyson
Oprah Winfrey
Peyton Manning
Robert Griffin III (RG3)
Stephen Colbert
Stephen Curry
Tom Holland
Zendaya

Library of Congress Cataloging-in-Publication Data
DiPrimio, Pete.
  Ben Simmons / Written by Pete DiPrimio.
    p. cm.
Includes bibliographic references, glossary, and index.
ISBN 9781624693397
1. Simmons, Ben. 1996- — Juvenile literature. 2. Basketball players—African American—Australia—Juvenile literature. 3. Philadelphia 76ers—NBA — Biography—Juvenile literature. I. Series: A Beacon Biography
  GV884.A45 2019
  796.32
[B]
                                                                Library of Congress Control Number: 2018943919
eBook ISBN: 9781624693403

ABOUT THE AUTHOR: Pete DiPrimio is an award-winning sports writer and freelance writer, and a member of the Indiana Sportswriters and Sports Broadcasters Hall of Fame. He has been an adjunct lecturer for the National Sports Journalism Center at IUPU-Indianapolis and for Indiana University's School of Journalism. He is the author of four nonfiction books pertaining to Indiana University athletics and more than two dozen children's books. Pete is also a recruiter for National Salvage & Service Corporation and a fitness instructor, plus a tennis, racquetball, biking, and weightlifting enthusiast.

PUBLISHER'S NOTE: This story has not been authorized or endorsed by Ben Simmons.

CONTENTS

Chapter One
Historic Beginning 5

Chapter Two
Early Years 9

Chapter Three
College Life 15

Chapter Four
Controversy 19

Chapter Five
NBA Opportunity 23

Chronology 26

Statistics 26

Chapter Notes 27

Further Reading 28

Books 28

Works Consulted 28

On the Internet 30

Glossary 31

Index 32

After five straight losing seasons, Ben Simmons (25) and All-Star teammate Joel Embiid sparked a dramatic turnaround for the Philadelphia 76ers for the 2017–18 season.

Chapter 1

Historic Beginning

Sometimes, special players thrive early. Ben Simmons is one of them.

The Philadelphia 76ers superstar rookie found a basketball mountaintop that LeBron James and Michael Jordan never could. Only NBA legend Oscar Robertson had gone that high before.

Nine games into his NBA career, Simmons was a triple-double equal with Robertson. Ten games produced numbers no one in the history of the game had ever achieved. And Simmons did this without mastering the outside jump shot.

Ben Simmons is a 6-foot-10, 230-pound Australian native who spent the beginning of his NBA debut season tearing up anyone who tried to stop him. In just nine games he recorded two triple-doubles (double digits in points, rebounds, and assists). Only Robertson, considered one of the 10 greatest players of all time, had done that in NBA history.[1]

By comparison, it took Michael Jordan 58 games to get two triple-doubles. It took LeBron James 118 games to do it. Both rate among the NBA's best ever.[2]

Simmons' ability to defend superstars such as Kevin Durant is almost as impressive as his offense.

According to the 76ers stat crew, Simmons was the only NBA player to ever total at least 170 points, 100 rebounds, and 80 assists in his team's first 10 games. That was in the fall of 2017. Not bad for a guy who missed the entire 2016–17 season with a foot injury.

People saw him as a freaky combination of LeBron James' speed and vision and Kevin Durant's agility and length. He was tall enough to see over anyone guarding him, explosive enough to get to the rim whenever he wanted, and aggressive enough to rebound his way into big plays.

And he was a point guard—not a point forward or a point center. He handled the ball well enough to run the show, and you'd better believe Philadelphia wanted him running it.

He could also play good defense, even against smaller guards. Very few big men are quick and athletic enough to do that. No wonder people kept comparing him to a young James.

Not everyone thought Simmons would be so good so fast, but he understood that to reach his potential, he had to work hard. James helped him. When he was 17 years old, Ben participated in the LeBron James Skills Academy in Las Vegas. James told him to meet him and fellow NBA superstar Dwyane Wade at a hotel gym at 6:30 the next morning. Ben was there and listened when, according to *Sports Illustrated*'s Lee Jenkins, James told him, "You have an opportunity to be better than me, but you can't skip steps. You have to do the work."[3]

Ben did the work, and he realized that plenty more remained.

Halfway through the 2017–18 NBA season, Ben was averaging 16.9 points, 8.5 rebounds, and 7.4 assists. His numbers would have been even better if he were a better outside shooter—he shot just 29.6 percent from 10 to 16 feet from the basket. He was 0-for-9 from three-point range.

Only two other NBA players averaged at least 16 points, eight rebounds, and seven assists—James and fellow superstar Russell Westbrook.

Simmons' instant NBA impact as a rookie reminded many experts of the start of the career of LeBron James, one of the greatest players in history.

Ben's bid to make the NBA All-Star team faced this reality: In the previous 20 years, only three rookies had earned All-Star honors. They were Blake Griffin (2011), Yao Ming (2003), and Tim Duncan (1998).[4] James didn't make it as a rookie, even though he averaged 20.9 points, 5.9 assists and 5.5 rebounds.

Ben was a big reason why, at the near halfway point of the season, Philadelphia had a 19-19 record. That was a huge improvement. Its records over the previous four years had been 19-63, 18-64, 10-72, and 28-54.

The team was also now one of the NBA's youngest. Three starters—Simmons, Joel Embiid, and Dario Saric—were 23 years old or younger. Eight players were younger than 29.[5]

The team's future was bright—and so was Ben's.

Simmons was born and raised in Australia. In the town of Melbourne, his father, Dave, once starred as an Australian professional basketball player.

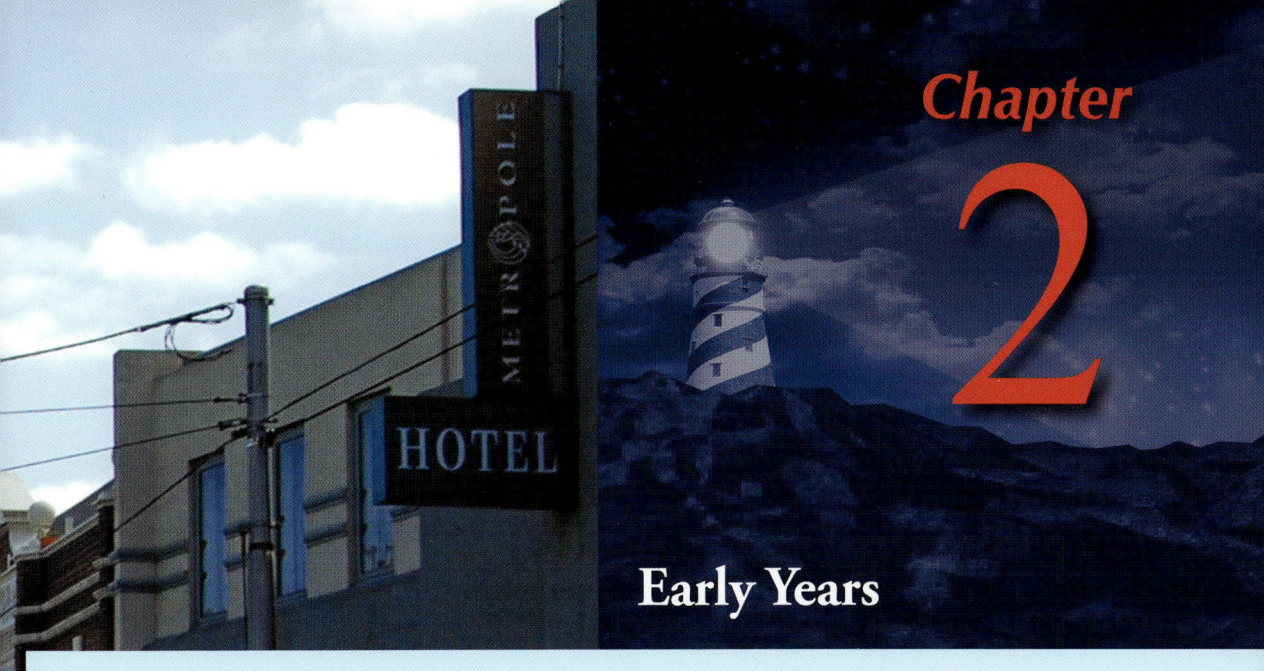

Chapter 2

Early Years

Benjamin David Simmons was born in Australia, in the small town of Fitzroy, a suburb of Melbourne. His father, Dave, was a 6-foot-9 American professional basketball standout who also played for 13 years in Australia's National Basketball League (NBL). He played U.S. college basketball at Oklahoma City before moving to Australia. Eventually he became an Australian citizen. He was a physical player good enough to be named an NBL All-Star and helped Melbourne win the 1993 NBL championship.

Ben's parents met in 1991. His mother, Julie, was an Australian aerobics instructor. She was a single mother with four children—Melissa, Emily, Liam, and Sean. She and Dave married in 1994 and had two children together, Ben and Olivia. The age difference between the oldest child (Melissa) and the youngest (Ben) was 15 years.

When Ben was 18 months old, his father began playing and coaching in the Australian town of Newcastle, on the Pacific coast. Within a few years, Ben was also playing, and playing very well. He showed guard skills—the ability to dribble, pass, and see the court the way smaller players did—at a young age. He even had a poster of NBA superstar guard Allen Iverson in his bedroom. When he wasn't playing basketball, he played tennis, bodysurfed in the Pacific, and ran along the beach with his golden retriever, Jasper.

When he was 7 years old, Ben began playing with and against much older boys for the Newcastle Hunters Under-12 team. Then he played for two older teams, Lake Macquarie and New Castle. He also played rugby, and like every sport he tried, he played very well.

The Simmons family moved back to Melbourne when Ben was 10, and he played junior basketball along with Australian Rules Football. He won awards—and championships—in both sports.

When he was 14, he decided to focus on just basketball. Why? He said it was because his Australian Rules Football coach wanted him to play a position called ruckman.

The ruckman is usually tall and athletic. It is one of the most important positions on

For a while it looked as if Simmons might become an Australian Rules Football player like these standouts– Archie Smith (in the air) and Jonathan Miles.

the field. His job is to control the ball during play stoppages, boundary throw-ins, and when the ball is thrown high into the air during something called center bounces. The problem is the ruckman often smacks into the other team's ruckman in nasty midair collisions. Simmons didn't want any part of that.

He did want to be a do-it-all basketball player like LeBron James, so he kept working on his ball handing and passing.

When he was 15 years old, in 2012, Ben earned a scholarship at the Australian Institute of Sports. Later that year, he traveled to the United States for the first time to participate in the Pangos All-American Camp. This camp invited some of the nation's best young players. Ben was able to participate because he was a citizen of the United States as well as Australia. He did so well that, for the first time, recruiters in the United States began to notice.

The next year, Ben played for Australia at the Under-17 World Championship. He helped Australia finish second and win a silver medal. Even though he was two years younger than everybody else, he dominated. Against the Czech Republic, he had 26 points, 10 rebounds, and five steals.[1]

Then it was time to go to high school. Ben decided to go to the United States so that he could play against some of the nation's best players. He picked Montverde Academy near

By the time Simmons had reached high school age, he was drawing attention from college coaches in the United States.

11

Orlando, Florida. He led Montverde to the High School National Tournament championship, then returned to Melbourne for more competition.

As a junior at Montverde Academy the next season, Ben averaged 18.5 points, 9.8 rebounds and 2.7 assists while shooting 69 percent from the field. He also blocked 88 shots. He led Montverde Academy to another National High School tourney title, and was considered the nation's No. 1 recruit among all high school junior players.[2]

Simmons continued to dominate as a senior. He was named the Naismith Prep Player of the Year, an award given to the nation's best high school

In the McDonald's All-America game, Simmons had no trouble getting to the basket, a sign of things to come.

player. He also was named the Gator National Player of the Year and a McDonald's All-American. He averaged 28.0 points, 11.9 rebounds, 4.0 assists, and 2.6 steals while leading Montverde to a third straight High School National Tournament title.[3]

Meanwhile, he continued to play on the Australian National Team.

Most national recruiting services rated him as the No. 1 high school player in America for 2015. He could have gone to any school, but there was one he liked more than any other, in part because his godfather, David Patrick, was an assistant coach there: Louisiana State.

Simmons' success at Montverde Academy in Florida earned him an invitation to the McDonald's All-America game, which is held annually for the nation's best high school seniors.

Simmons played his college home games at LSU's Pete Maravich Assembly Center. The facility is named for the former LSU All-American, one of the greatest college basketball players of all time.

Chapter 3

College Life

Ben arrived at Louisiana State University (LSU) and excitement soared. He was the highest rated player to come to LSU since NBA Hall of Famer Shaquille O'Neal in 1989. Fans expected Ben to lead the basketball team to the NCAA Tournament, and maybe make a run at a national championship.

On Instagram, O'Neal called Ben "the best player in the world."[1] Later, according to ESPN.com, O'Neal told Ben while they were taking a picture with young fans, "You're the man now, not me."[2]

LSU officials added to the excitement with a ticket-sales drive called "He's Coming," which showed Simmons' No. 25 uniform.

In a preseason overseas trip in August 2015, the LSU Tigers played five games in Australia. Ben was a sensation. In an 89-75 win over the Newcastle All-Stars, he had 22 points and 10 rebounds. The game was played at Newcastle Basketball Stadium, where his father had once played. LSU went 3-2 on the trip, with Ben averaging 20 points and nine rebounds.[3]

That got Tigers fans even more excited. Then Ben was named the Southeastern Conference's preseason player of the year (only the second freshman to get that preseason honor, joining Kentucky's Julius Randle from

Despite LSU coach Johnny Jones' positive approach, the Tigers couldn't play well enough, or win often enough, to make the NCAA Tournament with Simmons.

2013) and earned Associated Press preseason All-America recognition. LSU was ranked No. 21 in the Associated Press top-25 poll.

Ben's first official college game was a double-double success. He had 11 points and 13 rebounds as LSU beat McNeese State. The Tigers started 3-0 before losing to Marquette despite Ben's 21 points, 20 rebounds, seven assists and two steals.[4]

LSU began struggling, but Ben didn't. He had 43 points, 14 rebounds, seven assists, five steals and three blocks in a 119-108 win over North Florida. The 43 points were the most by a LSU player since Shaquille O'Neal had 43 against Northern Arizona in 1991.

Ben kept putting up big numbers. That included 14 points and 10 rebounds against national power Kentucky. In a pair of tweets, NBA Hall of Famer Magic Johnson compared Ben to a young LeBron James as a strong all-around player.

"LSU's Ben Simmons is the best all-around player I've seen since LeBron James came out of high school straight to the NBA," Johnson tweeted.[5]

And then, "Whatever team selects Ben Simmons will be getting a player that will have an immediate impact on their squad!"[6]

Ben was put on the midseason watch list for the Naismith Trophy, awarded every year to the nation's best college player.

However, Ben wasn't doing as well in the classroom, mostly because he didn't always go to class. Because of that, he didn't start against Tennessee.

By the end of the season, Ben was named SEC Freshman of the Year and made the all-conference first team. He averaged 19.2 points, 11.8 rebounds, 4.8 assists and 2.0 steals. He shot 56.0 percent from the field and grabbed 388 rebounds, the most in the Southeastern Conference. He scored as many as 43 points, and had at least 20 points in 18 games. He was a first-team All-American and was named the United States Basketball Writers Association of America's freshman of the year.

However, LSU went only 18-13 and did not make the NCAA Tournament. That was a big disappointment, given all the preseason excitement.

On March 21, 2016, Ben announced he would skip his final three years of college to enter the NBA Draft. He left school, signed with an agent (Rich Paul of Klutch Sports), and began working out to get ready.[7]

Ben had a connection to Klutch Sports, whose clients included LeBron James. Ben's sister Emily worked there.

That reflected how big sports are in the Simmons family. Emily had rowed for Washington State while in college. She married NFL player Michael Bush. Ben's brother, Liam, also played basketball and became an assistant basketball coach for Southwest Baptist.

As Ben prepared for the NBA, he got plenty of guidance from his father. Ben understood the challenge—and the opportunity. He was determined to take advantage of it.

Simmons never cared about being a good student at LSU. He did care about being a great player, and getting a shot to play in the NBA.

Chapter 4

Controversy

Ben did not go to LSU for the education. He went to LSU because NBA rules would not let a player enter the league draft right out of high school. Players had to wait a year, so Ben waited at LSU.

He and his family didn't like the "one-and-done" rule. They didn't think it was fair. They thought that players should have the right to start making a living as soon as they were ready, no matter the age.

Ben wasn't interested in getting a degree. He did just enough to stay academically eligible for the first and second semesters at LSU, but after December, he stopped going to class.[1]

His approach was highlighted in Showtime's 91-minute cable TV report called *One & Done*. The show follows Ben from his early days in Australia to his high school time in Florida, his days at LSU, and up to the 2016 NBA Draft. It shows the good, the bad, and the frustrated.

Ben's frustration included the time as an LSU freshman when he was buying bedding at a store. He used his debit card, and the ATM asked if he wanted cash back. He didn't have much money in his checking account, so he couldn't get any cash. If he had been allowed to play professionally, he would have had millions of dollars to spend.[2]

He also knew LSU was making a lot of money because of what he could do on a basketball court.[3]

As far as going to class, Ben didn't see the point. He knew he would turn pro as soon as the basketball season was over, and he didn't care that, by not going to class, he would hurt LSU's standing with the NCAA. Every school is required to show that its athletes are working toward graduation by taking and passing courses. Schools that can't show that their athletes are making progress can be penalized, including a loss of scholarships.

At one time during *One & Done*, Ben's sister Emily asks him, "Are you ever at school?" And then she says, ". . . it's like you're a full-time athlete."[4]

In many ways, he was.

The show also indicated that Ben didn't have many friends at LSU, and that he and his basketball teammates were not close. After he had 36 points and 14 rebounds to help the Tigers win at Vanderbilt, his teammates did not really celebrate with him. A lack of team chemistry was a big reason that LSU did not have a good season.

All this came while Ben was just 19 years old. He was learning how to handle all the attention, demands, and pressure. Like so many young people, he sometimes did not handle it well.

Simmons told *Sports Illustrated* during his NBA rookie season that he didn't think college prepared players for what life is like as a professional athlete. "Getting you ready to live that lifestyle," he said, "teaching you to take care of your money, take care of your body. If you're not going to pay them, at least pay them in that way."[5]

Simmons was finally getting paid. He made between $3.9 million and $5.9 million in his first season as part of his two-year guaranteed contract with the 76ers.[6] The contract was extended two more years, so he could make more than $26 million over the four-year total.[7]

Ben also signed a deal with the shoe company Nike. It would pay him between $20 million and $40 million.[8] He also signed contracts with Foot Locker, Beats by Dre, and Upper Deck.

Finally, he could get all the cash back he wanted.

That left him with one big goal—thriving in the NBA.

Simmons was more than a scorer for the Philadelphia 76ers. He got up close and personal while defending the Washington Wizards' Kelly Oubre, Jr.

Chapter 5

NBA Opportunity

Few NBA teams, including Washington, had the talent to match Philadelphia young guns Simmons and Joel Embiid.

Physically, Ben was ready for the NBA coming out of college, but some wondered if he had the right attitude after what had happened at LSU.

Philadelphia coach Brett Brown wasn't one of them. Brown was a former Australian NBL coach and a friend of the Simmons family. He had once coached Ben's father in Australia. The 76ers had the No. 1 draft pick and they were determined to take Ben.

First, though, they took a long look at Duke's Brandon Ingram. He impressed Philadelphia officials with a strong workout and was positioned to go No. 1.

Then Ben blew away the 76ers with an even stronger workout. Philadelphia drafted Ben on June 23, 2016, and Ingram had to settle for the No. 2 pick with the Los Angeles Lakers.

After the draft, in July 2016, Ben played well in the Las Vegas Summer League. He averaged 10.8 points, 7.7 rebounds, and 5.5 assists. He didn't shoot well, but he could pass, rebound, and make plays. Everyone expected him to have a shot at winning NBA Rookie of the Year honors.

Ben was set to play in the Olympics in Brazil in August 2016, but decided to pass and concentrate on his first season in the NBA.

Meanwhile, 76ers coaches couldn't decide if Simmons should play power forward, which would make him an inside player, or point guard, which

Brett Brown

would let him run the offense. Brown spent a lot of time with him, showing him videos of LeBron James and former superstar NBA guard Magic Johnson, who at 6-foot-8 was one of the biggest point guards ever. Simmons learned how to be a point guard.

On September 30, 2016, Ben was injured during a Philadelphia training camp workout. He had broken a bone in his right foot. Doctors said he'd miss three to four months. But the injury didn't heal right and team officials decided to hold him out until the next season. Ben told the *Philadelphia Inquirer* in July 2017, "Sitting out a whole year gave me a chance to really take a step back and look at the game and make sure I was focusing on the right things. And then, obviously, my body and taking care of my body and just continuing to work."[1]

By the fall of 2017, he was healthy and ready. Simmons instantly played like a future superstar. Yes, there were some glitches. He couldn't make free throws or three-point shots, and he struggled with any kind of outside jumper. Some wondered how well he would play with talented teammate Joel Embiid.

As it turned out, it was very well.

Ben is a left-handed shooter who shoots better with his right hand. During warmups he shoots with both hands. During games, he shoots layups and floaters with his right hand, but he shoots free throws and jumpers with his left hand, even though his right-handed shooting is better. During one workout, he hit a full-court shot while using his right hand. He once told reporters he wanted to shoot right handed, but his father made him shoot and dribble with his left hand.[2]

He struggled so much shooting free throws as a rookie that, in one game, the Washington Wizards sent him to the free-throw line a record 24 times in the fourth quarter. He made 15.[3]

Meanwhile, Ben was a 21-year-old superstar who, in a lot of ways, was still a teenager at heart. According to *Sports Illustrated*, he likes milkshakes, Sour Patch Kids (a soft, sugary candy) and interesting pets, such as Flash, his French bulldog. He also thought about wearing white basketball shoes (size-16 Nike Hyperdunks) because a Philadelphia trainer told him they would make him look quicker.[4]

Plenty of video work helped get Simmons ready for his rookie NBA season.

He even joined the Raise the Cat movement, for which people post photos of themselves holding up a cat. Raise the Cat shirts were for sale. It started after a 76ers win over Charlotte, when fans noticed Ben had posted Snapchat photos of his cats perched on his shoulders.[5]

Ben kept himself busy off the basketball court. For instance, during the 2017 holiday season, he starred in a cartoon called "Getting' Buckets with Ben Simmons." It was sponsored by Nike and Champs Sports. In this kids' cartoon, he talked about what it was like to join a new team with everybody expecting so much from him, and how he handled the foot injury that cost him his first season. The goal was to help young players face their own pressures.[6]

Ben also attended the opening of a new Police Athletic League center in Philadelphia. He wanted to inspire kids to use the facility, which includes a homework club and mentoring.[7]

Best of all, Ben would be going into his second season with a great honor. In June 2018, he won the NBA Rookie of the Year award, further cementing his place with the great NBA players of the past and the present.

CHRONOLOGY

1996 Benjamin David Simmons is born on July 20 in Melbourne, Australia.

2012 He plays on the Australia FIBA World U17 Championship silver-medal winning team

2013 He plays on the Australia/New Zealand FIBA Oceania Championship gold-medal-winning team.

On October 14, Ben commits to Louisiana State University (LSU).

2014 On November 12 Ben signs with LSU

2015 He is named the Gatorade National Player of the Year, Naismith Prep Player of the Year, McDonald's All American, first-team Parade All-American. He scores 36 points in Montverde win over Nevada Bishop Gorman High School in the Hoop Hall Classic in Springfield, Massachusetts.

2016 He is named first-team All-SEC, SEC Freshman of the Year, Associated Press First-Team All-American, USBWA National Freshman of the Year.

On June 23, Philadelphia selects Ben as the No. 1 pick in the NBA Draft. On July 2, he signs a multi-year contract with the 76ers that will pay him about $26 million over four years.

In late September, Ben hurts his right foot in practice. On October 4, he has surgery to repair a fracture in his foot. Estimated recovery time is 10 to 12 weeks.

On October 21, 76ers coach Brett Brown talks about Ben returning in January. The next day, Brown said he was wrong, that there is no date for Ben's return. On December 13, Ben starts shooting free throws without a walking boot.

2017 On January 10, Ben is cleared to begin participating in 5-on-0 drills. 76ers officials hope he can start playing in March. In February, an MRI scan reveals Ben's injury is not fully healed and he will not play this season.

2017 Ben makes his NBA debut on October 18 against the Washington Wizards and totals 18 points and 10 rebounds. He is named the NBA Rookie of the Month for November.

2018 Ben is named NBA Rookie of the Month for January and February.

Ben helps lead the 76ers to a third-place finish in the NBA Eastern Conference with a 52-30 record and a 16-game winning streak to end the regular season. They make the playoffs for the first time since 2012. Ben finishes the regular season with 38 double doubles and 12 triple doubles. He helps lead Philadelphia to a 4-1 opening-round playoff win over the Miami Heat. He averages 18.2 points and 10.6 rebounds in that series.

Ben is named NBA Rookie of the Year.

STATISTICS

Regular Season Stats

Season	Team	Games	Rebounds	Assists	Steals	Blocks	Points
2017-18	76ers	81	8.1	8.2	1.7	0.9	15.8

Playoffs Stats

Playoffs	Team	Games	Rebounds	Assists	Steals	Blocks	Points
2018	76ers	10	9.4	7.7	1.7	0.8	16.3

CHAPTER NOTES

Chapter One: Historic Beginning
1. Ward-Henninger, Colin. "Sixers Rookie Ben Simmons Joins Oscar Robertson in Elite Triple-double Club." *CBSSports.com*. October 24, 2017.
2. Marcin, Tim. "Ben Simmons Did Something Even LeBron (Or Anyone Else in NBA History) Hasn't Matched." *Newsweek*. November 8, 2017.
3. Jenkins, Lee. "The Process Is Over: Ben Simmons and the 76ers Have Arrived." *Sports Illustrated*. December 4, 2017.
4. Rosenblatt, Zack. "Will Sixers' Ben Simmons Actually Be Named an NBA All-Star?" *NJ.com*. January 5, 2018.
5. Jenkins.

Chapter Two. Early Years
1. "Simmons Stuns Czechs." *Sports TG* D-League. August, 2015. http://websites.sportstg.com/assoc_page.cgi?client=1-8876-0-0-0&sID=236246&&news_task=DETAIL&articleID=19816080
2. Keeble, Brett. Basketball Junior Ben Simmons Has World at His Big Feet. *Newcastle Herald*. June 30, 2014. https://www.theherald.com.au/story/2386842/basketball-junior-ben-simmons-has-world-at-his-big-feet/
3. Biancardi, Paul, and Mike Couzens. "Montverde Academy Wins Third Straight National Title." *ESPN.com*. April 8, 2015.

Chapter Three. College Life
1. ABC.net. "Ben Simmons the Best All-Around Player Since LeBron James: Magic Johnson." January 5, 2016.
2. O'Neil, Dana. "From Melbourne to Baton Rouge, Ben Simmons Has Arrived at LSU." ESPN.com. November 4, 2015.
3. Louisiana State Athletics. http://www.lsusports.net/pdf9/3733006.pdf?ATCLID=210284787&SPSID=27826&SPID=2166&DB_LANG=C&DB_OEM_ID=5200
4. Associated Press. "Marquette Uses Late Free Throws to Nip No. 22 LSU 81-80." *ESPN.com*. November 24, 2015. http://www.espn.com/ncb/recap?gameId=400827731
5. Twitter: Earvin Magic Johnson. January 5, 2016. https://twitter.com/magicjohnson/status/684528296537620481?lang=en
6. Twitter: Earvin Magic Johnson. January 5, 2016. https://twitter.com/magicjohnson/status/684529549753729024
7. Forbes. "Klutch Sports on the Forbes Sports Agencies List." 2017. https://www.forbes.com/companies/klutch-sports/

Chapter Four. Controversy
1. Norlander, Matt. "One and None: The Paradoxical Legacy of Freshman Ben Simmons' LSU Career." *CBSSports.com*. February 24, 2016.
2. Parrish, Gary. "76ers Rookie Ben Simmons' Year at LSU Exposed in Showtime's 'One & Done.'" *CBSSports.com*. November 4, 2016.
3. Ibid.
4. Ibid.
5. Jenkins, Lee. "The Process Is Over: Ben Simmons and the 76ers Have Arrived." *Sports Illustrated*. December 4, 2017.

CHAPTER NOTES

6. Zucker, Joseph. "Ben Simmons, 76ers Agree to Contract: Latest Details, Comments and Reaction." *Bleacher Report.* July 2, 2016.
7. Fox Sports. "Philadelphia 76ers Announced They Will Take Up the Third-Year Option of Ben Simmons' Rookie Contract." November 1, 2017.
8. Zillgitt, Jeff. "How Nike Landed Shoe Deal with No. 1 Pick Ben Simmons." *USA Today.* June 28, 2016.

Chapter Five. NBA Opportunity

1. Cooney, Bob. "Sixers' Ben Simmons Benefited From His Year Off the Court." *Philadelphia Inquirer.* July 10, 2015. http://www.philly.com/philly/sports/sixers/ben-simmons-sixers-process-year-off-injury-joel-embiid-20170710.html
2. Kalbrosky, Bryan. "Ben Simmons Is Likely Better Shooting Free Throws with His Other Hand." *Hoops Hype.* November 30, 2017.
3. Ibid.
4. Jenkins, Lee. "The Process Is Over: Ben Simmons and the 76ers Have Arrived." *Sports Illustrated.* December 4, 2017.
5. Carson, Dan. "Ben Simmons Joins Sixers Fans in 'Raise the Cat'." *Foxsports.com.* January 21, 2017.
6. Johnson, Jeff. "Ben Simmons Stars in New Nike x Champs Sports Animated Holiday Campaign." *Bleacher Report.* December 21, 2017.
7. Todd, Sarah. "Sixers Ben Simmons and Amir Johnson Help Unveil PAL Center in Strawberry Mansion." *Philly.com.* September 7, 2017.

FURTHER READING

Books

Bryant, Howard. *Legends: The Best Players, Games and Teams in Basketball.* New York: Puffin Books, 2017.

Christopher, Matt. *On the Court with ... Stephen Curry.* New York: Little, Brown & Co., Hachette Book Group, 2017.

Editors of Sports Illustrated Kids. *Big Book of WHO Basketball.* New York: Sports Illustrated Kids Big Books, 2015.

Zuckerman, Gregory. Elijah Zuckerman. and Gabriel Zuckerman. *Rising Above: How 11 Athletes Overcome Challenges in Their Youth to Become Stars.* New York: Philomel Books, 2017.

Works Consulted

ABC.net. "Ben Simmons the Best All-Around Player Since LeBron James: Magic Johnson." January 5, 2016. http://www.abc.net.au/news/2016-01-06/ben-simmons-the-best-all-round-player-since-lebron-magic/7070708

FURTHER READING

Arnovitz, Kevin. "You'll Never Believe the Oblong Ball Behind Ben Simmons' Genius." *ESPN.com*. December 14, 2017. http://www.espn.com/nba/story/_/id/21769248/nba-how-australian-rules-football-made-ben-simmons-best-rookie-lebron

Biancardi, Paul, and Mike Couzens. "Montverde Academy Wins Third Straight National Title." *ESPN.com*. April 8, 2015. https://web.archive.org/web/20150412223154/http://espn.go.com/video/clip?id=12618204

Carson, Dan. "Ben Simmons Joins Sixers Fans in 'Raise the Cat'." *Foxsports.com*. January 21, 2017. https://www.foxsports.com/nba/story/philadelphia-76ers-ben-simmons-raise-the-cat-joins-sixers-fans-in-raise-the-cat-is-a-national-treasure-012117

Fischer, Jake. "Reexamining the Simmons vs. Ingram Debate." *SI.com*. December 19, 2017. https://www.si.com/nba/2017/12/19/ben-simmons-brandon-ingram-lakers-76ers-2016-nba-draft-comparison

Forbes. "Klutch Sports on the Forbes Sports Agencies List." 2017. https://www.forbes.com/companies/klutch-sports/

Fox Sports. "Philadelphia 76ers Announced They Will Take Up the Third-Year Option of Ben Simmons' Rookie Contract." November 1, 2017. https://www.foxsports.com.au/basketball/nba/ben-simmons-thirdyear-team-option-picked-up-by-76ers-while-jahlil-okafors-contract-was-not/news-story/d7ac11fd3a0dd820a7eaafe6b8e9123e

Jenkins, Lee. "The Process Is Over: Ben Simmons and the 76ers Have Arrived." *Sports Illustrated*. December 4, 2017. https://www.si.com/nba/2017/11/30/ben-simmons-philadelphia-76ers-lebron-james-the-process

Johnson, Jeff. "Ben Simmons Stars in New Nike x Champs Sports Animated Holiday Campaign." *Bleacher Report*. December 21, 2017. http://bleacherreport.com/articles/2750517-ben-simmons-stars-in-new-nike-x-champs-sports-animated-holiday-campaign

Kalbrosky, Bryan. "Ben Simmons Is Likely Better Shooting Free Throws with His Other Hand." *Hoops Hype*. November 30, 2017. http://hoopshype.com/2017/11/30/ben-simmons-is-likely-better-shooting-free-throws-with-his-other-hand/

Marcin, Tim. "Ben Simmons Did Something Even LeBron (Or Anyone Else in NBA History) Hasn't Matched." *Newsweek*. November 8, 2017. http://www.newsweek.com/ben-simmons-did-something-lebron-michael-jordan-havent-matched-stats-706041

Norlander, Matt. "One and None: The Paradoxical Legacy of Freshman Ben Simmons' LSU Career." *CBSSports.com*. February 24, 2016. https://www.cbssports.com/college-basketball/news/one-and-none-the-paradoxical-legacy-of-freshman-ben-simmons-lsu-career/

O'Neil, Dana. "From Melbourne to Baton Rouge, Ben Simmons Has Arrived at LSU." *ESPN.com*. November 4, 2015. http://www.espn.com/mens-college-basketball/story/_/id/14050003/from-melbourne-baton-rouge-ben-simmons-arrived-lsu

FURTHER READING

Parrish, Gary. "76ers Rookie Ben Simmons' Year at LSU Exposed in Showtime's 'One & Done.'" *CBSSports.com.* November 4, 2016. https://www.cbssports.com/college-basketball/news/76ers-rookie-ben-simmons-year-at-lsu-exposed-in-showtimes-one-done/

Prada, Mike. "Ben Simmons Is a New NBA Species Who Bends the Game to His Will." *SBNation*.com. December 22, 2017. https://www.sbnation.com/2017/12/22/16810454/ben-simmons-film-breakdown-76ers-pradas-pictures

Rosenblatt, Zack. "Will Sixers' Ben Simmons Actually Be Named an NBA All-Star?" *NJ.com.* January 5, 2018. http://www.nj.com/sixers/index.ssf/2018/01/will_sixers_ben_simmons_actually_be_named_an_nba_a.html

RotoWire Staff. "76ers' Ben Simmons: Near Triple-double in Wednesday's Win." *RotoWire.* November 16, 2017.

Sharp, Andrew. "The Ben Simmons Injury and the Bigger Picture for the Sixers." *SI.com.* October 3, 2016. https://www.si.com/nba/2016/10/03/76ers-ben-simmons-injury-foot-fracture-sam-hinkie-bryan-colangelo

Todd, Sarah. "Sixers Ben Simmons and Amir Johnson Help Unveil PAL Center in Strawberry Mansion." *Philly.com.* September 7, 2017. http://www.philly.com/philly/sports/sixers/philadelphia-76ers-sixers-pal-center-strawberry-mansion-ben-simmons-20170908.html

Ward-Henninger, Colin. "Sixers Rookie Ben Simmons Joins Oscar Robertson in Elite Triple-double Club." *CBSSports.com.* October 24, 2017. https://www.cbssports.com/nba/news/sixers-rookie-ben-simmons-joins-oscar-robertson-in-elite-triple-double-club/

Zillgitt, Jeff. "How Nike Landed Shoe Deal with No. 1 Pick Ben Simmons." *USA Today.* June 28, 2016. https://www.usatoday.com/story/sports/nba/2016/06/28/nike-shoe-contract-no-1-pick-ben-simmons/86491236/

Zucker, Joseph. "Ben Simmons, 76ers Agree to Contract: Latest Details, Comments and Reaction." *Bleacher Report.* July 2, 2016. http://bleacherreport.com/articles/2649837-ben-simmons-76ers-agree-to-contract-latest-details-comments-and-reaction

On the Internet

LSU Men's Basketball: Ben Simmons
   http://www.lsusports.net/ViewArticle.dbml?ATCLID=210041987

NBA.com.: Ben Simmons.
   http://www.nba.com/players/ben/simmons/1627732

GLOSSARY

aerobics (ah-ROH-biks)—Any type of exercise that increases heart rate and lung power.

assist (uh-SIST)—A play in which one player passes the ball to another player, who then makes a basket.

Australian Rules Football (aw-STRAYL-yin ROOLS FUT-ball)—A contact sport that is like American football except that each team has 18 players on the field at a time, instead of 11.

floater (FLOH-ter)—A shot taken inside the lane with the player jumping into the air and softly shooting it.

Olympic Games (oh-LIM-pik GAYMZ)—A competition that features multiple sports, happens every four years, and involves athletes from all over the world.

one-and-done—To stay in college for only one year and then leave for the NBA.

point forward (POYNT FOR-werd)—A large offensive player who has the size to move inside and the skill to play like a guard.

point guard (POYNT GARD)—The player who runs a team's offense. He makes passes, gets teammates in the right position, and is like a coach on the court.

Police Athletic League (puh-LEES ath-LEH-tik LEEG)—An organization in many police departments in which officers help coach boys and girls in sports and help them with homework and other activities. The goal is to build character, keep kids out of trouble, and help the police stay on good terms with the community.

potential (poh-TEN-shul)—Something that is possible.

rugby (RUG-bee)—A British game that is like a cross between soccer and American football.

SEC—Southeastern Conference

team chemistry (KEH-mis-tree)—The way players on a team get along and like each other. The more team chemistry you have, the more likely that team will win.

triple-double (TRIH-pul-DUH-bul)—The act of getting double digits (at least 10) in three different categories, usually points, rebounds and assists or steals.

PHOTO CREDITS: Cover, pp. 1, 4, 6, 7, 18, 21, 22, 25—Keith Allison; p. 8—Ramira, Nicholas Boullosa; p. 10—Flickerd; pp. 11, 12, 13—Tony the Tiger; p. 14—Daniel Foster; p. 16—the Jumper 3; p. 24—Tasty Poultine. Every measure has been taken to find all copyright holders of material used in this book. In the event any mistakes or omissions have happened within, attempts to correct them will be made in future editions of the book.

INDEX

Brown, Brett 23, 24
Charlotte Hornets 25
Czech Republic 11
Duncan, Tim 7
Durant, Kevin 6
Embiid, Joel 5, 7, 23, 24
Fitzroy 9
Griffin, Blake 7
Ingram, Brandon 23
Iverson, Allen 9
James, LeBron 5, 6, 7, 11, 16, 17, 24
Johnson, Magic 16, 17, 24
Jones, Johnny 16
Jordan, Michael 5
Klutch Sports 17
Lake Macquarie 10
Las Vegas 6, 23
LeBron James Skill Academy 6
Louisiana State University 13, 14, 15
Melbourne 8. 9, 10, 12
Miles, Jonathan 10
Ming, Yao 7
Montverde Academy (Florida) 11, 12, 13
Naismith Trophy 12, 17
NBA All-Star Team 7
Newcastle, Australia 9, 10, 15
Newcastle Basketball Stadium 15
Nike 20, 25
Oklahoma City 9
O'Neal, Shaquille 15, 16
Orlando 12
Oubre, Kelly Jr. 21
Pangos All-Star Camp 11
Patrick, David 13
Paul, Rich 17
Philadelphia 76ers 5, 6, 7, 23, 24, 25
Police Athletic League 25
Raise the Cat 25
Randle, Julius 15–16
Robertson, Oscar 5
Saric, Dario 7
Simmons, Ben
    awards 11, 12, 15, 16, 17
    birth 9
    charity 25
    draft 17, 23
    education 11–13
    siblings 9
Simmons, Dave (father) 9
Simmons, Emily (sister) 9, 17, 20
Simmons, Julie (mother) 9
Simmons, Liam (brother) 17
Simmons, Olivia (sister) 9
Smith, Archie 10
Sour Patch Kids 25
Wade, Dwyane 6
Washington Wizards 24
Westbrook, Russell 7